THE JOURNEY AND OTHER TITLES

THE JOURNEY AND OTHER TITLES

Poems and Parables

NEHEMIAH BOSTICK

Rising Word Publishing, LLC
P.O. Box 340242
Brooklyn, NY 11234

Printed in the United States of America

First Printing, 2017

ISBN-13: 9780692826850
ISBN-10: 0692826858

Library of Congress Control Number: 2016963481
Rising Word Publishing LLC, Brooklyn, NEW YORK

CONTENTS

Faith · 1
The Journey · 3
The Master · 4
The Blacksmith · 6
The Identity · 7
The Runner · 8
The Runner's Creed · 9
The Knocking (Temptation) · 10
The Conversation (Forgiveness) · · · · · · · · · · · · · · · · · · 11
The Legacy · 13
Death · 14
The Storm · 16
Q&A · 17
The Savior · 18
The Name (Jesus) · 19
The Thought · 20
The Battle (Spiritual Warfare) · 21
The Table · 22
The Rock (Luke 19:40) · 23
The Accountability · 24

The Valley · **25**
The Crucible · 27
Empty Swing · 28
Stack of Cards · 29
A Dream or Two · 30
The Boxer (12th Round) · 31
The Adversity · 32
The Tenacious · 33
The Cadet (C4C) · 34
The Lost (Where to Find Myself) · 36
The Doubt · 37
The Lust · 38
The Grief (of Sin) · 39
A Warning · 40
Character · 42
Black-on-Black Crime · 43
Night and Day · 44

Love and Nature · **45**
The Dawn · 47
Heavenly Father · 48
For M · 49
The Flower · 50
The Woman · 51
The Worth (To Young Women) · 52
Flower Petal · 53
Fall to Winter · 54
The Moon's Song · 55
Mommy · 56
Numbers · 57
Friendship · 58
The Strength (To Young Men) · 59
A Moment · 60

For Whom the Heart Beats · 61
To You · 62
The Wait · 64
The Dusk · 65

Parables · **67**
The Theme Park · 69
The Faithful Servant · 73

Thanks! · **77**

FAITH

THE JOURNEY

What is this journey that I am on?
So many mountains to climb.
So many valleys to tread.
All I see is the way.
Such a long way to go.
Will I ever arrive? Will I ever cease to grow?
I am never ready. I am never set.
Always uncomfortable. Always vulnerable.
Pain. Such pain in the depths of my soul.
Can you see the scars?
To rest but never to stop. No, never to stop.
Walking this road. Walking through time.
I have seen so much, yet I have seen nothing.
My mind. Oh, my mind, it is breaking.
Lord, give me strength, for I lack understanding.
Failure I chase. And success, success I leave behind.
Never to do it again. Never to repeat time.
Oh! My God, tell me, please. What is the purpose?
What is the plan? Your ways are too high.
Your thoughts too grand. Lord, help me.
What is this journey that I am on?
I cannot do this alone. I am only
Only just a man.
So please lead me on this journey.
On this journey that I am on.
For I am just a breath.
And in a moment. Yes, just a moment.
My life will be gone.
Oh! What is this journey that I am on?

THE MASTER

To be a slave bound and led
Is to be every man's fate,
Whether alive or whether dead
Who is thy master the question is cast
To the many, to the first, and to the last
What is their name, and where do they lead the voice calls aloud
Each to give an answer, from the humble to the proud

I have no master, a man cries
   Another voice speaks, yes, but that's a lie
   I am your master and king over haughty eyes
   My name is Pride, and I lead to where the lowly lie

One man shouted, I do not know, with a voice of anger
   A reply came, but that's not true, for you and I are not strangers
   I am your master, and I cast out peace from life
   My name is Rage, and I lead only to violence and strife

A few men mumble, what does it matter, we won't live to see tomorrow
   A voice whispers, who knows, but for now, I am your master,
   And my name is Sorrow
   I lead to broken spirits and joyless laughter
   Where thoughts only dwell on death and disaster

Many men proclaimed, we don't care as long as we fulfill our desires
   Several voices answered,
   We are your masters and promise they will never transpire
   For we are Gluttony, Lust, and Greed
   And we lead to the empty, the shallow—the forever in need

Some men don't give a reply, their tongues too heavy to speak
> A tired voice stumbles out, I am your master,
> And I am lord of the weak
> My name is Sloth, and excuses are my lot
> I lead to poverty, hunger, and death—where life begins to rot

Within the midst of the shameless, the shackled, and the bound
A man awaiting his turn answers with a confident sound
> I know my Master; yes, I seek His face
> He leads me to still waters with mercy and grace
> He is Righteousness, Truth, Joy, and Love
> He sits enthroned, at the right hand, far up above
> My Master's name is Jesus, as you can see
> Yes, my Master's name is Jesus. The only one to rule over me!

THE BLACKSMITH

Can you hear Him working?
Tirelessly working.
In the heat He labors.
By the light He crafts.
Melting hardened hearts.
Purifying darkened souls.
With firm hand and gentle touch,
He fashions His beloveds.
Striking and folding.
Heating and molding.
He makes them all new.
And glory. Such glory
Will be seen by the works
Of His hands.

THE IDENTITY

Who told you who you were? Who said you had to be that?
Who told you to go there? Who said you needed to do that?
Don't listen to them. Definitely don't listen to that!
They just want to limit you, to deceive and shackle you in fact.
Neither do they know your purpose, nor do they know your plan
That is too vast for them. Too great for any angel, beast or man.
I AM the one that made you. You were knit by my loving hands
For you to know me; to walk with me hand in hand
To go where I lead you. To hear my voice and listen to my command.
You are priceless, holy, and made righteous
Royalty has adorned you! Don't ever think your life is worth less
You are my child, and I am your Father.
You are my child, so know and remember, you don't have to look any farther
You are a child of the Everlasting God, so trust it will ever be so.
You are a child of the Most High God, and that is really all you need to know.

THE RUNNER

I will run...
Yes, a race that has already begun
A race that is full of burdens and strife
A race that is itself life.
To run through rain, thunder, and snow
To run even when I don't know where to go
To stumble, to fumble, and even to fall
To run to rise, to run to give all.
When breath is weak and muscles tire
When bones crack and lungs fill with fire
Even when cursed with bile, venom, and spit
I will not stop; indeed, I will not quit.
To run until this race is done
To run into His arms and hear, "Well done."
Yes. I will run.

THE RUNNER'S CREED

I will run
When the race gets hard, and the road looks long
I will run
When my body gets weary, and my muscles ache and bones shake
I will run
When I stumble and fall, and thoughts come just to end it all
I will run
When every breath is agony, and others say my life is a tragedy
I will run
When I can't see the light, and darkness comes and fills me with fright
I will run
When others ask why, and I don't have a reply
I will run
When the storms come and seek to wash me away
I will run
When the burdens become too great, and my life seems at stake
I will run
When sweat is lost, blood is spilled, and dreams are gone
I will run

To you LORD I will run, because you are my strength
To you LORD I will run, because you give me grace
To you LORD I will run, because Father I am desperate

Desperate to hear you say, "Well done."

THE KNOCKING (TEMPTATION)

A constant perversion knocks at my door
Calling in whispers that creep along the floor
It calls my name, seeking—
Wanting and wishing, it craves for more (me)
To come and answer that deplorable knock
That is knocking at my door.

It speaks of deceit and breathes out lies
But still I pace, with tightly shut eyes
I pace that soul-laden floor
That lies between me and the creature
The creature that is knocking,
Knocking at my door.

Louder they grow and louder still
These knocks that are banging on my door
These knocks that are breaking down my will
With each knock, my heart to beat faster and faster
Oh, Faustus! Was this your warning of the coming disaster!

Searching for my Master, yearning for His grace
Calling His name. Seeking His face!
For as it grows more and more
To realize only He can stop this evil knocking
Knocking at my door.

THE CONVERSATION (FORGIVENESS)

Hey, God, are you out there? I want to ask you something.
There is this rumor going around that you are into forgiving.
But I don't think that could be so.
For if you knew what I did, you could never let it go.

- "Not true, and I do know."

Wait! Really? Even when you've seen the report?
The report on how many times I fell short.
On how many times your Word was neglected.
On how many times your Name was disrespected.
On how many times you said go, and I wouldn't.
On how many times you said stop, and I couldn't.
On how many times I didn't even try.
On how many times you watched with sad eyes.
On how many thoughts that were just downright vile!
On how often I walked around in denial.
On how many times I didn't acknowledge your grace.
On how many times I didn't seek your face.
Could you really forgive all this wickedness, rebellion, and sin?
Would you really, truly, let me in?

- "Yes."

But why, God? Why would you give me a clean slate?
With deeds this dark and sin this great.
I have not earned this. Why should I receive such a gift?

- "Because I love you, and I wanted to mend this rift."
- "Yes, your misdeeds spread far and wide."
- "But because I love you, trust me, you don't have to hide."
- "Forgiveness and redemption are mine alone to give."
- "Accept it. I love you. Come back to me and live!"

THE LEGACY

I was cast in perfection, with life breathed into me
Fearfully and wondrously I stood, flawless and pure, forever to be
Called to subdue, made to rule, and designed under authority
Until deception provoked discontent to be my enemy
A rebellious heart within. A blameless soul without
Truth sounded, and I was summoned to give an account
I had fallen; my own desires did I satisfy
But to take responsibility, no, my mouth didn't even try.
To blame the one under my care,
If I were to fall (in cowardice and weakness), then this burden I would share
To be cast out and laden with pain and strife
To suffer the consequences of sin, to lose this life
I was condemned, and out of my actions death did grow
To be passed on, generation to generation, death all would know
This would be the legacy that came from my hand
This would be the legacy of me, the first man.

DEATH

This is the story of the rise and fall.
Of one who came to take it all.

The son of rebellion. Born of discontent.
His presence a consequence of man's descent.
His purpose just. What man's wages had bought.
So he ushered in pain, sorrow, and rot.
Claiming the high and taking the low.
He claimed to reap what sin did sow.
To the many, one and all.
None could stand, and all did fall.
Reaching to the corners far and wide
He over took all in his stride.

But little did he know that there was one.
One who could renew all he had done.
He who is King and would conquer all.
He who in love would see him fall.

And conquered he was. Overcome on that fateful day.
That day when Christ said, "It is finished."
And washed Man's sins away.

And when Christ rose, making it complete.
There he could only stand in bitter defeat.
Knowing that all he had that made men cower.
Was reduced to nothing. Now, he had no power.
Because Christ rose, what was lost now was found.
Because Christ rose, now none could be bound.

And as we come to the end of the story.

I will leave with this and encourage you not to worry.

All who are in Christ need not fear Death and his misery.

For if you are in Christ, be assured you have the victory!

THE STORM

Lightning flashes! Blinding as quick fingers tear at the sky,
Heralding thunder's laughter as it echoes off the world's edge,
Revealing a fearsome Humor (to one who is magnificent).
In the raging gust, wind's breath howls and moans.
It speaks warnings, secrets to the still ear.
And as the sky weeps, the bitter deluge floods the soul
Drowning peace in its misery.
For in the power that is the drama of the tempest
Lies the fear of one who is mighty to save.

Q&A

"Time ticks and tocks.
We live and die.
But what do we do
when time stops?"

    "When time stops, look for He
        who lived and died for thee.
        And who rose again. For He is
        for whom time stops."

THE SAVIOR

For to call out to the one who is able
It is not within me;
For my lips are stained by unclean speech!
But in His mercy and grace, He rescues me
With pierced hands and bloody brow
He lifts me up.
And as I am carried in His arms,
Cleansing blood flows over me
From the side that was pierced.
And in His presence, all my bonds break.
I am made righteous
For my Savior is the Lamb that took my place,
Slain for me.

THE NAME (JESUS)

Hello, gentlemen. Pardon my interruption.
But I really need to ask you a question.
Do you know the Name?
The Name that is above all names?

The Name that makes the enemy cower.
The Name that is a strong tower.

It is the Name that makes the demons flee.
It is the Name that sets the captive free.
A name that if it is near, then you won't have to fear.

Do you know the Name that is forever great?
The Name that is never late.
It is a name that leads to still waters.
The Name that makes orphans sons and daughters.

It is the Name that created time and space.
The Name that is full of love and grace.

It is the Name that bled for me and you.
A name that will forever be true.

So if you know this Name, please tell me.
For I am desperately seeking, you see.
Seeking to know this Name.
For I heard it can take away all my sin.
And all my shame.

THE THOUGHT

To think is to be. As such, it
Which makes us wondrous creations
Rules us and conducts our
Every move. Like a symphony,
We play to each stroke it sends creeping
Through our minds. It alters, corrupts, revolutionizes,
And frees us...An infinite paradox.
It loves and wars against itself
In the same continuous space.
Our greatest enemy and most beloved friend.
To be nothing, yet worth everything,
Purely a precious entity. For in itself it is
Us.

THE BATTLE (SPIRITUAL WARFARE)

Colossal foes encompass
With insidious smiles, they attack
In the secret places...
Thoughts not to think
Feelings never to express
The sowers of wicked seeds
Nemeses naught of flesh and blood
Seeking to ensnare the Soul
In agony
Cries sound out!
Closing eyes to an enemy unseen
Falling on humble knees
To clothe in the full armor (of God)
With the Sword of the Spirit—
Drawn from grace-cleansed lips
To battle! To stand! To never lose the fight!

And in the presence of the LORD
I will fear not!

THE TABLE

There is a table in my heart
Full with many seats,
Clothed in much splendor
The LORD at the head.
He passes peace, gives grace,
And bestows favor
On my soul.
That He would dwell with me
And show His Love...
My heart to sing His praises!

To each seat, a patron
And each patron, a gift
My heart to burst
From such prosperity.
That my table be laden
With love and favor.
The foundation cannot be moved!
Who am I to dine
In the company of such
Majesty?

THE ROCK (LUKE 19:40)

Can you hear my voice? Can you hear my cry?
You who give no praise. You who don't even try.
To be a fool with a heart of rebellion, eyes for thine own glory.
If you have ears to hear, you better heed this story.
I am the rock, and I have been assigned to you,
Created by the Maker, to cry out when you refuse to.
I only stay silent when you learn to take a stand.
When you learn to praise God and lift up empty hands.
For such is the Glory of God that His name must be praised.
It cannot be held back. It won't be captured. It won't be caged.
And if your lungs don't let out the praise as they breathe
If your lips refuse to set the reverence free
Then I am declared to shout and declared to sing
Declared to praise our God in mystery.
For who am I to praise our God
When He gave me no breath for sound
And who are you not to, when He gave you everything?
From the sea, to the sky, to the ground.
For if the day comes and I am singing as your sun sets
Beware the tears of shame, for they will be wept.
And eternity will be where you reflect
On how you answered this choice.
Should I be silent, or should I lift my voice?

THE ACCOUNTABILITY

You did not take the food out of my hand.
But did you ever put some in?
You did not strip me naked.
But did you ever put clothes on when I was?
You did not put me in jail.
But did you ever visit when I was within?
You did not make me cry out for help.
But did you ever hear when I did?
You did not speak death to me with your tongue.
But did you ever encourage with the word of Life?
You did not send me down the wrong path.
But did you ever point to the right one?
You did not deceive me with lies.
But did you ever speak about the Truth?
Many wrongs you did not commit.
But is there much good that you did omit...?

THE VALLEY

THE CRUCIBLE

Can you feel the heat?
The flames! They burn.
Hotter and hotter still.
My Soul. My mind. My heart.
They melt against the rage.
Agony. Oh, the agony that I feel.
It consumes me. And wretchedness
What wretchedness has come!
I am made known, and it rises.
It ascends from the depths.
Dross from my bones.
Dross from my heart.
It is scraped from my being.
It is scraped from my soul.
Unmade, I am poured out...

And He will fashion me.

EMPTY SWING

I'm so lonely! Won't anyone play with me?
I sit on a swing, a sad sight to see
All alone I sway back and forth, dreaming
Of the day I can cast off this feeling
This feeling of sadness and despair
That continuously strikes my soul as I stare
At this empty swing next to me
Longing to fly and swing free
To have that space filled with a warm face
Would light my soul and give me joy—

But for now, I will sit and swing alone

STACK OF CARDS

Gently I stack these feeble cards
That represent my fragile being
Made from my heart's scattered shards
To struggle in their guard is a battle never ceasing

And as diamond stacks on spade
In the ever upward climb to the top
I wish these cards of stone had been made
For in such would have my heart stop

To not feel such pain and agony in life
That these cards would quiver at a simple touch
My soul to cry out in such strife
And watch delicate cards bear too much

—Crumbling, these simple folds fall beneath my soul

And as I lie in weeping sorrow
I pick up my heart of cards
And begin again for tomorrow

A DREAM OR TWO

It's nice to have a dream or two
One for me and one for you.

Do not dream of the past,
For then your dreams will never be new
And do not dream too small,
For then your dreams will be too few
But do pray that your dreams come true
For if not, you will only say sad and blue
That you used to have
A dream or two.

THE BOXER (12TH ROUND)

As bloody sweat drips from my chin
I hear the bell ring and then ring again.
Looking up in the opposite corner
I see a beast, not a man, approaching in ravenous hunger.
He swings with his left. He swings with his right
I say a quick prayer, pleading to make it through the night.
Bobbing and weaving, I try to keep pace
Desperation starts to set in, and my heart begins to race.
Remember what you practiced; remember what you learned, I say to myself
As I continually dodge these punches that wish to diminish my health.
Strategies dart through my mind as I hear the corner yell,
"Left, left, right, upper, come on boy, give 'em hell!"
I hit him with a jab, which only seems to make the beast madder
I throw a quick hook and start to flee so as not to climb Jacob's ladder.
He launches furious blows that seem to cleave the air,
Ducking and diving, he misses my chin just by a hair
I hit the body and throw two uppers. His knees buckle
Sensing I might have a chance, I start to chuckle.
"Don't get cocky!" I hear someone scream, "He's not out yet!"
I think, "A few more punches and I may take that bet."
The clack, clack, clack announces the remaining ten
I look at the beast and brace myself to go in
I swing with my left; I throw out a right; hell, I swing with all my might
And just as I throw my greatest punch, the ref steps in, and that's the fight.
It's over. My fist just inches from victory…and his face.
I exhale exhaustion and loss from my lungs as I bow my head
And see my gloves hang in the empty space.

THE ADVERSITY

Your path will not be easy
And your burden will not be light!
In this game of life (where souls are the pieces)
Woes shape the board
And motives become strategies.
I will not be overlooked!

You will feel my presence and take heed.
To take me lightly will instill your doom,
For I will not go quietly into the night!
My will is strong and shall not be broken easily.
For I am he who rages and claws for the victory.
He who stands on the fallen.
You will not overcome my pride with simple grace.
Only in deep-rooted effort, painful toil,
And gritted strife will you find my defeat.
And in this, you shall find yourself
And know that you are
So much more…

THE TENACIOUS

I fall on bended knee in a field of shattered dreams.
Hands, dead, hang limp at bruised sides.
Head bowed, under the laced crown of failure.
Tears of agony descend, muddying the earth.
Upon sunken shoulders lays the cloak of regret
My back, burdened with the yoke of disappointment.
I am bones broken, flesh torn, grief flowing through hollow veins.

But!

I will rise and ascend again.
For in my soul burns the flame of desire
And in my mind lies the sting of defeat.
I will emerge from the ashes with strength and power.
With torn hands, regain everything taken
And in my triumphant march, you will
Know Me!

THE CADET (C4C)

My rights have been willingly and forcefully taken
The heart and mind have been mercilessly broken
Cynicism has become my cover
Bitterness and hatred have taken over
Why am I here? The question that keeps calling
I think of no answer while I am crawling
Through this life of a four degree
I take in breath while I try to see
The hope that shines in the darkness
But that light, folly, as I choke in this harness
Suffocating between dueling emotions
While people try to comfort with their simple coercions
I want to go, but I can never leave
Because wasted time I do believe
Will send you back with misery—in both your eyes
And will leave you asking why, why, why...
To struggle on, I try my best
Looking on in the direction west
Those mountains seeming so beautiful, high, and risen
But, really, they are my hated prison
Below them the civilians laugh and play
While I, above, watch them and pray
To my God, who loves and cares for me
Why has He brought me to this place of misery
I don't think I will ever know

Until I graduate from this hell with snow
So I sit here trying to feel better
Listening to people and reading their letters
But it doesn't seem to get easier, only harder
So I will trust my God
My heavenly Father

THE LOST (WHERE TO FIND MYSELF)

Do you know where to find me? For I do not
I think I was lost somewhere behind a thought.
I looked for my place in the book called life
But constantly turning the pages caused nothing but strife.

Checking through the years, I think I might have shown my face
But after year eighteen, I got lost in the empty space.
I thought to look in the mirror and ask my reflection
But that plan only led to hopeful deception.

To look to others to help find me was just silly
For whatever they would find would cease to be me.
And it saddens me not to have myself by my side
For without him, my true self can only hide
And wait, hoping that someday I come along
To take back the life that I should love,
Which wouldn't be so wrong.

So if you happen to see me in the street, passing through
Please wish me a how do you do
And let me know that I need to get back.
Get back, so I can set my life on the right track.

THE DOUBT

It grips my heart with steel claws
Sinking them into its depths
It looks to devour my sanity, my very soul
Ripping through skin, muscle, and bone
I scratch to free this dark creature
From my cage of flesh
To my sorrow and shame, I am rendered incapable
Its fiendish smile stares at my broken will
Its sickening laugh echoes throughout my mind.
Like a plague, it infects my whole being
And I coolly drown in the sinful pit of its existence.
Who will save this wretched Soul?

THE LUST

I see beautiful women on all sides.
Their sensual shapes assaulting
My eyes with pleasure.
Strutting by with confident strides
My heart leaps from within me!
My mind scorches
With dreams and fantasies.
Carnal urges start to traverse.
Through my veins
Desire bites into my heart
And pierces my sanity with ravenous hunger.
And yet my soul is distraught.
Knowing Truth…

It burns!

THE GRIEF (OF SIN)

To believe a lie
To forsake the Truth
To live to die
To waste one's youth

To lose the Way
To be chained
To have to pay
To forever be pained

To walk in darkness
To never see Life
To eat bitterness
To drink strife

To stumble and fall
To reject the hand
To ignore the call
To cease to stand
To end it all

A WARNING

What emotions must run
Through a feeble mind
As desolate eyes consume the world

For in it lies the wicked king
Head adorned with lies
Never sleeping, never ceasing
To devour is his pride

The wisdom of the ages
Held in esteem spouts nothing
But inane dreams.
With hands that touch gold (cast by fools)
And feet that trample sorrows

With only pale, sick breath
And false hope
Would tomorrow you so desire
For tomorrow holds no life for you
Who serve the king of iniquities and wants

Sounds of gnashing
And howls of wailing
Echo in the ears
Of those who bow to the created
Feeding on the beguiling words
Of the trickster

It is the living Word you should crave
For it is the spring of life
And in these somber words so spoken
For to find a hint of light
Take heed
For your soul
To not fuel the fire

CHARACTER

Are you an honest man, dear sir
Or do you lie through your teeth?
Are you a kind man, dear sir
Or are you ruthless beyond belief?
Do you seek justice, dear sir
Or do you hold hands with hypocrisy?
Do you walk with righteousness, dear sir
Or do wicked fools keep you company?
Are diligence and discipline your teachers, dear sir
Or do you let sloth be your guide?
Are you a faithful man, dear sir
Or is adultery your true bride?
Is peace your kinsman, dear sir
Or is your blood filled with anger?
Do you listen to prudence, dear sir
Or do you court danger?
Are you a humble man, dear sir
Or do you worship pride?
Do you know the measure
Of your character, dear sir?
Please answer these questions,
Then decide.

BLACK-ON-BLACK CRIME

Oh, I hate my brother!
Yes, I hate him, as you can see.
For he is nothing.
Yes, nothing. Only pure misery.
So I will bruise him
I will break him.
Defile him
And misuse him.
Deceive him
And confuse him.
Yes, I will kill him
And forget him.
I'll do much worse
Than you could ever.
And I'll do it
With simple pleasure.
And should you ask me why
With a sad, weeping eye.
I'll tell you
In simplicity.
I hate my brother.
Oh, yes, I hate him.
Because he
Is really me...

NIGHT AND DAY

Day, why do you oppress your brother Night?
What has he done that he should feel your might?
His purpose is noble and his value no less (than yours).
Why do you curse him with your lips when they were created to bless?
Day, you should help your brother Night, for he is needy and poor.
Teach him what you have learned. Sharpen him; make him more.

Night, why do you rage against your brother Day?
Even when he wrongs you, do not hate him, or keep him at bay.
Love him. Embrace him, even when it may be a bitter gall.
Be noble. Be righteous, so in your integrity you may stand tall.
And shed light on your brother's injustice if he should commit it.
Teaching him the folly and shame of his ways, so he may shun it.

Night and Day, you are brothers. You should not cause the other strife.
You were made to support each other. To lift each other up in life.
Don't believe the lie of prejudice and discord. Walk in truth, hand in hand.
So all the stars may see that Love, yes, Love, can heal this broken land.

LOVE AND NATURE

THE DAWN

It rises out of the east
Splitting darkness across the horizon.
A new day's blood crawls over the world's edge
Igniting the heavens in an orange hue
While yellow fingers grasp at the never-ending sea
And as the blinding eye rises to the stage
Darkness, searching for sanctuary, reaches to the shadows
And with its arrival, life is reborn.
And in its majesty, His glory shines for all to see
For in His presence, there is a blessing that is untold
A beauty unseen, a song unheard, a love unimaginable.
For as the day breaks, time starts anew
And our Genesis can be seen.

HEAVENLY FATHER

Who am I that I should see your glory LORD?
You bless me and lead my feet from strife.
In your statutes, I take refuge, for they lead me to peaceful water.
I praise your name, LORD, in my secret place;
For you are good, and your love endures forever.
You place your hand over me and comfort me in my days of longing.
You give me favor with men and still my enemies.
When I stumble, you pick me up again and dust my sin from me.
LORD, you are my blessed Redeemer.
Glory to God in the highest.
Your wonders captivate my very breath.
The works of your hands, my tongue cannot express
The magnitude of their greatness.
Your beauty I cannot fathom.
For all that you have done, for all that you do, and for all that you will do
I will praise you, LORD.
My God, I will exclaim your praise forever!
Amen.

FOR M

My love is near
And my heart trembles.
Her beauty outshining the brightest star
Who am I to deserve such wondrous devotion
For her love is as deep as the ocean
Her kisses are sweet nectar
Her touch, silk to my skin.
What deed have I done to be blessed
By such a love.
I am unfit for her gaze, her thoughts, her care
But the God that is and is to come
Has given me this divine blessing, through my love
And in all her wonder, she takes joy in my company
For I delight in hers ever so.
She is my beautiful addiction
She is my companion, my lover, my friend.
Such grace is given from on high that I may
Delight in the walk with my love,
Through life,
Her loving hand in mine.

THE FLOWER

What makes you beautiful?
The sweet scent, vibrant colors,
Your shape? Or are you beautiful
Because you are simply you?
My Flower. My Love.

THE WOMAN

God's beautiful gift
Loyal friend and terrible foe
Compass for when he strays
Humility for his ego
Seductive temptress
Strength when he is weak
Comforter. Supporter.
A smile for his frown
Elegant and graceful Queen
His known treasure
Star in the night sky
His sugar pie
His love
His blessing

THE WORTH (TO YOUNG WOMEN)

Dear young woman, do you not know your worth?
The LORD has declared this since before your birth.
You are a dove that is worthy of love and to be loved.
Through Christ's blood, you are royalty and worthy of loyalty.
You were created one of a kind and are worthy of a man's faithful mind.
The LORD made you beautiful and calls you to be discrete,
You are worth so much more than wide eyes, gaping mouths,
And whistles in the street.
Declared priceless through the Son by the Father, you were made for one,
Not many.

Dear young woman, you are worth all of a man. Anything less is pennies!
Claim your worth as a bride
Never settle to be a woman on the side.
You are a gem, the apple of your Father's eye.
Do not put up with men who know not your worth
With those who don't even try.
Know your worth, young woman, as declared by the Word
And if you should be challenged and told some fancy lies
Remember these truths you have heard
And listen to the words of the wise.

FLOWER PETAL

For whom do you smile so sweetly
Longing for the touch of your love
Overlooking the green meadow
Waiting for your dearest to return
Ever waiting, ever loving
Reaching out with soft fingers

Pleasing to the eyes
Everlasting beauty
The Sun's lover
Aphrodite's messenger
Lover's gift

FALL TO WINTER

As the morning star sets himself to sleep
Autumn lays his cool blanket over the earth so green
And as the leaves close their eyes for slumber
Their brown, orange, burgundy, and auburn smiles
Fill my soul with utmost wonder
And when they float down to lay their heads on the crisp grass
The trees, naked and proud, stand waiting for winter's cold kiss.

Winter's frozen fingertips gently drape across the land
Through the night's jewel-studded sky,
The trees are clothed in her white splendor
White robes carefully woven in depressed clouds
Each stitch an unparalleled and unique flake
Dressed in white cloth, the trees are majestic in their stance
And as the morning star wakes, his smile lights the world
The trees, strong and firm, stand in their bright glory
As the light dances along Winter's white crystals.

THE MOON'S SONG

The setting sun lights my face to gleam
To see myself in your depths is but a dream
You dance to the earth's steady heartbeat
Melodic waves that are simply too sweet
An untamable mistress
Would I wish for only a kiss
But to give my heart would be to cease living
For in your nature, your love is fleeting
Full of passion and wonder
You sweetly tear hearts asunder
Yet full of life you be
And to all, you are the key
You show us who we are
Even reflecting the brightest star
Seductive, wild, and free
Your beauty will always be a sight to see

MOMMY

Soft cheeks the color of chocolate
Warm embraces
That melt away the coldest depression
A love that is unquestioned
A gift to the one given to you
Wonderful blessing from He who reigns
Loving unashamed
Forever mine

NUMBERS

What to do with only one,
To think this might be fun.
   It could be split and become two.
But just as red is not blue, two just will not do.
   How about three, that would be nice?
Yes, three is a good number, but it still would not suffice.
   What about four, really, who could ask for more?
Me, I could ask for more, and really, four is just a bore.
   Five, that would not be too bad.
Yes, yes, but five sounds a little sad.
   I got it; six, six could be your number.
I don't know, that would cause me to wonder.
Why not seven, eight, or nine?
Wait, that's it, nine; nine will suit me just fine.
   OK then, why not ten?
Aw, man, now we have to start all over again.

FRIENDSHIP

To look into the eyes and view love that stretches from the soul
To feel an embrace that pulls through adversity
It sets my feet to move

My voice never to fall on deaf ears
My feelings never to be under heavy feet

Rays of light when confusion clouds
Sound judgment accompanied with sweet wisdom

To bestow upon my shoulders the world and her woes
To trust in me with secrets and sadness

A blessing in her truest form
With a heart that weeps for my pain
A firm pillar never to be forgot

THE STRENGTH (TO YOUNG MEN)

Dear young man, do you not know your strength?
You struggle, claw, and scratch. Why do you go to such lengths?
You were made to rule. Under God in humility.
You are a king under the King of kings. Stop chasing futility.
Stop abdicating your responsibility. And your right.
It is for you to lead. For you to stand. For you to fight.
You are to be the glory of God. Walking in His wondrous might.

Dear young man, please heed these words, and don't lose sight.
You are called to be a protector. A provider. A priest.
You are royalty, a son of God. Don't live as lesser men or a beast!
Rule your domain with wisdom, righteousness, and confidence.
Trust, as a man of integrity, you have the blessing of Providence.
And should you be favored to receive a queen
(Yes, just one!) to help you rule.
Please. Please! Love her as Christ does, and don't be a fool.
For she is your sister in Christ. Royalty.
A favored daughter, don't you know?
Do not treat her as a slave, a tool, or worse…a five dolla' ho.
For she is one with you (especially after that night)
And brings much to the table.
So don't dare believe the lie of ignorant arrogant men,
Who would say she isn't able.
Respect her. Value her. Love and keep her. And she will do the same.

Dear young man, enjoy the life the Lord has given you.
Rejoice! Remember where your strength comes from
And rule your world in His name.

A MOMENT

May I have a moment of your time?
So I can tell you all these secrets that are mine.
Some are light and free; some are dark with despair.
I would love if you could just lend me your ear.
And please, do not shrink back in fear.
For these secrets are only meant for the heart of a true friend.
So come close, dear friend, and let not this time come to an end.
To share my love, hate, and precious desires.
So you see, to find a friend to listen is most dire!
For the Grave is beckoning and the Bell tolling.
So allow me to speak candidly while my eyes are closing.
Remember me, dear friend, as my life fades away.
Don't let my memory go as night breaks to day.
Remember me, dear friend.
At least until…
Your dying day.

FOR WHOM THE HEART BEATS

My love forever grows
For the flower that
Blooms softly in the
Stillness of my heart
Casting its beauty to the
Horizon

TO YOU

To you whom I have yet to meet,

With this simple pen and fragile heart
Let me tell you of the love that is yours.
Let yourself peer through my eyes
And view the magnificence
That I look upon in my dreams.
When such radiant and pure eyes look upon me,
Should my heart not burst from joy
That overflows with every beat?
Your voice, the sweet melody
That brings peace to my soul.
To see your smile
Is to see the sun rise in the East.
It cast my fears asunder.
Your curves flood my eyes with yearning.
The taste of your kisses,
The sweetest of honey cannot compare.
They set fire in my bones!
Your simple touch
Takes breath from my lungs.
Your caress steals my air.
My thoughts are captivated
By your very essence.

I am yours and yours alone.

So, my love, do not forsake my hand when we meet.
For in it lies
All my Heart.

THE WAIT

Oh, my lovely bride. My Queen.
Hear your King, and know I am unvarnished.
I have waited for you with a pure longing.
Unsoiled am I. Body kept sacred for you.
For your honor, I stand among men an outcast.
I have conquered not. No pearls have these lips kissed.
No mountains have these hands scaled.
No gardens have these feet trod.
I have chained desire in my heart.
Ravenous hunger lay shackled in my soul.
To defraud no man. To defile no lady.
I have waited for you. By Grace I have waited.
And unto you, only you, will I lay myself bare.
Body, mind, and soul will be made known to you.
And, my Queen, my beautiful bride, know this truth.
I have waited for you and will continue to wait.
I just request, my Love, humbly request
That you wait for me too.

THE DUSK

It sinks down into the shining sea,
Drowning into tomorrow.
And as Forever strikes
A path that speaks to His glory—
Sky is cleaved from sea.
Yellow rays burn auburn and simmer red
My soul shouts! Extoling Truth's name.
If only to begin to comprehend such beauty
Would my heart leap for my first Love
And laughter be placed on my tongue.
For when darkness creeps in its wake
And stars begin to dance
Around that fading light,
May my lips not speak ill but marvel at
The works of His hands.

PARABLES

THE THEME PARK

There is a theme park open to the public. At the park, you'll find the greatest ride you could ever ride. There is none better. The line is long and the wait grueling, but the ride is definitely worth it. You see people come out, and they come out changed. They are still the same people with the same clothes but...still different. Their walk is different. Their talk is different. Even their attitudes are different. In fact, you notice that the people who went on the ride who weren't smiling before are walking out with smiles. And the ones who actually were smiling have smiles that are twice as big. Aside from all that, the biggest thing you notice is that everyone who comes out from the ride starts sharing and telling people about the ride. They say with amazement that the others should definitely go on it, too. They say the ride is crazy good, totally awesome, and that it won't disappoint!

As you continue to watch, you notice the actions and reactions of the many people passing by the ride. Some notice the long line and are discouraged and upset. They express that they definitely don't want to wait that long. So they pass by the ride and don't look back. They head toward the other rides that are certainly less thrilling but have shorter lines and, most importantly, will fulfill their desires now.

Others pass by the ride and notice the line, but they also notice the people coming out from the ride. They stop to consider getting in line but ultimately decide to move on and come back later. They say that maybe when the line is shorter they will come back at the end of the day.

You then notice the people who pass by the ride and see the people coming out and decide without hesitation to get in line. You hear them chatter that the ride must be good because the line is so long. You hear them urge others to check it out and give it a go. And when these people come out from the ride, you see the same change in them as in the others who rode the ride before.

As the day progresses and news about the ride is shared, more and more people start to get in line. Even some of the people who passed by the ride at first, having heard the testimonials of the riders, come back and get in line. But you also notice that even as the day wears on, not everyone is getting in line.

You look around and of course notice the many folks telling others about the ride and its wonders and greatness. But you observe that there are different reactions to the riders and their testimonies. You see some shake their heads and laugh at the riders. They say they don't really care about the ride, no matter how great it is. You hear some even say that the other rides are just as good and have shorter lines, so they will stick with them instead. These people walk away from the riders.

You notice others having lengthy conversations with the riders, asking for more details and about what makes the ride so great. After these conversations, you see some people look intrigued, and they walk over to the ride. Others are no more different than when the conversation began, and they say that they'll check out the ride later—but not now.

Then you see others who, after hearing about the ride and how great it is, run over to get in line. Some even leave the lines they were already in.

And as the day continues to wear on, as it does, you notice something peculiar. Some of the people standing in line for the greatest ride are leaving—before having gone on the ride. The people staying in line plead with them to stay. They're almost there! But you see that the people leaving just shake their heads. Some leave saying they're tired and don't want to stand anymore. Others claim that staying in line is silly, and that they could have ridden many other rides by now. They're going to go join the others and do what they want.

You see some of those still in line question the wait and wonder if they should leave, too. But the others firmly hug the ones questioning and turn them to face the end of the ride so that they can see the others coming out and be reminded. The wait is worth it, they tell them, encouraging them and keeping them in line.

As the day finally comes to a close and you watch darkness creep over the sky, an announcement goes out over the park. It states that the theme park is closing, and the time for fun is at an end. It says that everybody in line for any ride can finish the ride, but no one else can join a line anew.

So once all the rides finish their lines, the Owner of the theme park comes out to see everybody exit the park. But before all could get in their cars, the Owner gives an announcement for all to hear. The park is having a special celebration—a grand event called Park after Dark. You hear Him state that all rides will be open and all amenities paid for in full. Special bands and guest performers will be there, and the park will put on a dazzling light show.

You see all the people get excited and notice how they can't wait to get back into the park. But there is a caveat, the Owner says. The celebration event is only for those who rode the greatest ride. He states that the greatest ride is not just great because it is the best ride in the theme park. It is also great because, more importantly, it is the only way to get an invite to the Park after Dark celebration. For only after waiting in line and riding the ride were you told about the event and given a wristband.

With this revelation, you notice the start of much grumbling and complaining from within the crowd. Someone speaks the question, "Why can't those who didn't go on the ride during the day go now and get an invite so they too can join in the celebration?"

To this the Owner replies: "Did not all of you have an opportunity to get in line to ride the greatest ride when the park was open? Did not all of you pass by and see the ride? The line? The riders coming out who rode the ride? And, if you came in from another entrance, were you not told about the ride? And even for those who were in line when the park closed, did I not give time for everyone in line to finish and complete the ride?"

Amazed, you see that all those in the crowd become silent. For all that the Owner says is true. Then the Owner continues: "I am sorry, my friends, but the time for the celebration has arrived. Would it be just or fair or true to my Word if I delayed my promise to those who rode the ride when they were told after seeing and hearing of its glory? Would that be just when they had the same opportunity as you? No, unfortunately you rejected the greatest ride, my friends, and now you have to go."

And with that you see the Owner, with joy on His face, escort all who had ridden the great ride back into the park where there is much feasting, joy, and celebrating. But you also see, with much wretchedness and sorrow, that those who did not ride the great ride are left outside with saddened and downcast faces.

THE FAITHFUL SERVANT

One day, a servant went to his Lord and asked if he could do great things for his kingdom. He had dreams of being a doctor. What could be better than being the one to heal the Lord's people? He also had thoughts of being a general. How great of an honor would it be to lead the Lord's armies into battle and victory? He even had musings of being a grand architect and engineer. Who could not be proud after constructing great buildings in the Lord's kingdom? All this and more he explained and told to his Lord. And when he was finally done, his Lord replied. He was glad that the servant had a heart for great things. But for now, all the Lord needed of him was that he do what was asked of him and do it well. That would be enough. With this, the servant went away dismayed. All his dreams for greatness in his Lord's kingdom would not be realized. But the servant still loved his Lord, so he would do as he was asked.

One morning, the Lord asked the servant to plant some seeds and tend the field in which the plants would grow. The servant obeyed, for he loved his Lord. But, still, the servant was sad. He had never dreamed of tending crops. That afternoon, the Lord came and asked the servant to tend and keep his horses, and the servant obeyed. Again, he loved his Lord. But, still, the servant was sad, for He had never imagined that he would be tending horses for his Lord. Later that evening, the Lord came a final time and asked the servant to dig up stones from the quarry and to cut them into squares. At this the servant's heart all but broke. He had never thought of stone cutting, even in his nightmares. But because he loved his Lord, the servant obeyed.

Each day, the Lord came to his servant and asked him to do these three tasks—morning, noon, and night. Each day, the servant obeyed. He did each task and did it the best he could, for the servant loved his Lord.

As time wore on, days turned into months, months into years, and years into lifetimes. The Lord's kingdom and lands flourished and grew. It became the most known kingdom throughout all the lands. And still the servant did as he was asked. He tended the fields, kept the horses, and cut the stone.

Then one day, the servant went to his Lord and asked if he could rest from his duties. He had now grown old, weary, and frail. He was no longer able to do what he was asked. But before the Lord answered his servant, he asked why the servant looked so sad and dismayed. The servant replied that a long time ago, when he was young and strong, he had dreams of doing great things for his Lord. But those dreams never came to pass. His whole life was now spent, and all he had done for his Lord was tend fields, keep horses, and cut stone. He had done nothing great for his Lord and now never would. At this, the Lord laughed. The servant became perplexed. He did not see how this situation was funny. And then the Lord said, "You, servant, are my most treasured of men. For you are my faithful servant. Out of your love and obedience, you have done many great deeds for my kingdom." The servant did not understand why the Lord would honor him with such words. All he had done was what was asked, and that was nothing more than tend fields, keep horses, and cut stone.

Then the Lord told him of the true merit of his work: how his crops were used as medicine to save thousands of lives and thousands still, how his horses came to fashion a cavalry known and feared throughout all the lands, and of how each stone he cut formed every building, tower, and monument within the kingdom. The Lord explained that if not for the servant and his faithfulness, the doctors would have been unable to heal, the armies unable to conquer, and the architects and engineers unable to build.

With that, the Lord took a ring, placed it on his servant's hand, and embraced him, saying: "Oh, my faithful servant, most treasured among men. Trust that you have done great things for your Lord. Come now, and rest in my home. For though you think not, be assured that you have done the greatest deed of all. You have been faithful and obedient to the end."

THANKS!

First, I give thanks to the Lord because He gave me the means, heart, and desire to do this, not to mention the inspiration. And I have to thank everyone who supported me and encouraged me to do this. Love and favor are really great things.

And to you, the reader, thank you for reading my book. I hope you were either encouraged, were entertained, were moved to think, found something to relate to, or—heck—had all of the above happen. But, overall, I do hope you enjoyed the read and found it interesting. As you can see, I love the Lord Jesus Christ and am so thankful He has been with me every step in my brief journey so far. I don't know where I'd be without Him. But I do, with my heart, encourage you to dig into Jesus and really learn what He's about and how He loves you (if you don't know already). Try Him; you won't be disappointed!

Be blessed and encouraged!

www.ingramcontent.com/pod-product-compliance
Lightning Source LLC
LaVergne TN
LVHW091230080426
835509LV00009B/1232